Artificial Intelligence In Business

A Practical Guide to Leveraging AI and Machine Learning for Competitive Advantage

By Lydia Carrington

Table of Contents

Chapter 1: Introduction to Artificial Intelligence and Machine Learning

Understanding the Foundations of AI in Business

1.1 Understanding Artificial Intelligence

1.1.1 What Is Artificial Intelligence?

Artificial Intelligence (AI) refers to the simulation of human intelligence processes by machines, especially computer systems. These processes include learning (the acquisition of information and rules for using the information), reasoning (using rules to reach approximate or definite conclusions), and self-correction. In essence, AI enables machines to perform tasks that typically require human intelligence.

1.1.2 The Evolution of AI

The concept of AI has evolved significantly since its inception in the 1950s. Early AI research focused on problem-solving and symbolic methods. In the 1980s, the field shifted towards statistical models and machine learning, emphasizing data-driven approaches. The advent of big data and enhanced computational power in the 21st century propelled AI into new realms, enabling breakthroughs in image recognition, natural language processing, and autonomous systems.

1.1.3 Types of AI

- **Narrow or Weak AI:** Designed to perform a specific task, such as virtual personal assistants (e.g., Siri, Alexa).
- **General or Strong AI:** A theoretical form of AI that possesses the ability to understand, learn, and apply its intelligence to solve any problem, much like a human being.
- **Super-intelligent AI:** A level of intelligence surpassing that of the brightest and most gifted human minds.

1.2 Machine Learning: The Core of Modern AI

1.2.1 Defining Machine Learning

Machine Learning (ML) is a subset of AI that focuses on the development of algorithms that enable computers to learn from and make decisions based on data. Rather than being explicitly programmed to perform a task, ML systems recognize patterns and learn from experience, improving their performance over time.

1.2.2 How Machine Learning Works

At its core, machine learning involves feeding data into algorithms and allowing the system to adjust and improve. The basic steps include:

1. **Data Collection:** Gathering relevant data from various sources.
2. **Data Preparation:** Cleaning and organizing data for analysis.
3. **Choosing a Model:** Selecting an appropriate algorithm for the task.
4. **Training:** Allowing the model to learn from the data.
5. **Evaluation:** Assessing the model's performance.
6. **Deployment:** Implementing the model in a real-world environment.
7. **Monitoring and Maintenance:** Continuously refining the model based on new data.

1.2.3 Categories of Machine Learning

- **Supervised Learning:** The model is trained on labeled data, learning to predict outputs from inputs.
  - *Examples:* Classification (spam detection), regression (predicting prices).
- **Unsupervised Learning:** The model finds patterns in unlabeled data.
  - *Examples:* Clustering (customer segmentation), association (market basket analysis).

- **Reinforcement Learning:** The model learns by interacting with an environment, receiving rewards or penalties.
  - *Examples:* Robotics, game AI.

1.3 Deep Learning and Neural Networks

1.3.1 Introduction to Deep Learning

Deep Learning is a subset of machine learning inspired by the structure and function of the human brain's neural networks. It utilizes layered structures of algorithms called artificial neural networks to model complex patterns in data.

1.3.2 Understanding Neural Networks

- **Neurons and Layers:** Neural networks consist of interconnected nodes (neurons) organized in layers—input, hidden, and output layers.
- **Forward Propagation:** Data moves through the network from input to output layers, undergoing transformations.
- **Activation Functions:** Mathematical functions that determine the neuron's output, introducing non-linearity.
- **Back-propagation:** The process of adjusting weights and biases based on the error rate obtained in the previous epoch (iteration).

1.3.3 Applications of Deep Learning

- **Computer Vision:** Image and facial recognition, autonomous vehicles.
- **Natural Language Processing (NLP):** Language translation, sentiment analysis.
- **Speech Recognition:** Virtual assistants, voice-controlled systems.

1.4 The Role of Data in AI

1.4.1 Importance of Data Quality

Data is the lifeblood of AI and machine learning. High-quality, relevant data is essential for training effective models. Poor data quality can lead to inaccurate models and flawed insights.

1.4.2 Data Types

- **Structured Data:** Organized in a fixed format, such as databases and spreadsheets.
- **Unstructured Data:** Includes text, images, audio, and video, lacking a predefined structure.
- **Semi-Structured Data:** Contains tags or markers to separate elements but not organized in a rigid structure.

1.4.3 Data Preparation Process

1. **Data Collection:** Gathering data from various internal and external sources.
2. **Data Cleaning:** Removing inaccuracies, duplicates, and irrelevant information.

3. **Data Transformation:** Converting data into a suitable format or structure.
4. **Feature Engineering:** Creating new input features to improve model performance.

1.5 AI in Business: An Overview

1.5.1 The Impact of AI on Business Operations

AI technologies have the potential to transform business operations by:

- **Enhancing Efficiency:** Automating routine tasks reduces time and resource consumption.
- **Improving Decision-Making:** Data-driven insights enable more informed strategic choices.
- **Personalizing Customer Experience:** Tailoring products and services to individual preferences.

1.5.2 Key Business Functions Benefiting from AI

- **Marketing and Sales:** Predictive analytics for customer behavior, targeted advertising.
- **Supply Chain Management:** Demand forecasting, inventory optimization.
- **Human Resources:** Talent acquisition, employee engagement analysis.
- **Finance and Accounting:** Fraud detection, automated bookkeeping.

1.6 Benefits and Challenges of AI Adoption

1.6.1 Benefits

- **Competitive Advantage:** Early adopters can outperform competitors by leveraging AI capabilities.
- **Cost Reduction:** Automation leads to lower operational costs.
- **Innovation Opportunities:** AI opens new avenues for product and service development.

1.6.2 Challenges

- **Implementation Costs:** High initial investment in technology and talent.
- **Data Privacy Concerns:** Managing sensitive data securely and ethically.
- **Workforce Disruption:** Potential job displacement and the need for reskilling.

1.7 Ethical and Legal Considerations

1.7.1 Ethical AI Practices

- **Transparency:** Being open about how AI systems make decisions.
- **Fairness:** Ensuring AI does not perpetuate biases or discrimination.
- **Accountability:** Establishing responsibility for AI-driven outcomes.

1.7.2 Compliance with Regulations

- **Data Protection Laws:** Adhering to regulations like the General Data Protection Regulation (GDPR).
- **Industry Standards:** Following sector-specific guidelines and best practices.

1.8 Case Study: AI Transforming Customer Service

1.8.1 Background

A multinational retail company sought to enhance its customer service operations, aiming to improve response times and customer satisfaction while reducing costs.

1.8.2 Implementation

- **Chatbots and Virtual Assistants:** Deployed AI-powered chatbots to handle routine inquiries.
- **Natural Language Processing:** Enabled the system to understand and respond to customer queries effectively.
- **Integration with CRM Systems:** Provided personalized responses based on customer history.

1.8.3 Results

- **Improved Efficiency:** Handled 60% of customer inquiries without human intervention.
- **Enhanced Customer Satisfaction:** Reduced average response time from hours to seconds.

- **Cost Savings:** Lowered operational costs by 25% due to reduced reliance on human agents.

1.9 The Future of AI in Business

1.9.1 Emerging Trends

- **AI and IoT Integration:** Combining AI with the Internet of Things for smarter devices and systems.
- **Edge Computing:** Processing data closer to the source for faster decision-making.
- **Explainable AI:** Developing AI systems whose actions can be easily understood by humans.

1.9.2 Preparing for Continuous Change

Businesses must:

- **Invest in Talent:** Develop skills internally or hire experts in AI and data science.
- **Foster a Culture of Innovation:** Encourage experimentation and adaptability.
- **Monitor Regulatory Developments:** Stay informed about changes in laws affecting AI use.

Chapter 2: The Business Case for AI

Leveraging Artificial Intelligence for Strategic Advantage

2.1 The Strategic Importance of AI in Business

Artificial Intelligence (AI) has transitioned from a futuristic concept to a practical tool that offers significant competitive advantages. Organizations across industries are exploring AI to enhance efficiency, drive innovation, and improve customer experiences.

2.1.1 Market Drivers for AI Adoption

- **Technological Advancements:** Increased computational power and the availability of big data have made AI technologies more accessible.
- **Competitive Pressure:** Companies adopting AI can outperform competitors by optimizing operations and creating new revenue streams.
- **Customer Expectations:** Modern consumers demand personalized services and rapid responses, which AI can facilitate.

2.1.2 Aligning AI with Business Strategy

Integrating AI requires alignment with the organization's overarching goals and objectives.

- **Vision and Mission Compatibility:** AI initiatives should support the company's long-term vision.
- **Strategic Objectives:** Identify how AI can help achieve specific targets, such as market expansion or cost reduction.
- **Cultural Fit:** Foster an organizational culture that embraces innovation and change.

2.2 Identifying Opportunities for AI Implementation

Successful AI integration begins with pinpointing areas where AI can add the most value.

2.2.1 Operational Efficiency

- **Process Automation:** Automate repetitive tasks to free up human resources for strategic activities.
- **Resource Optimization:** Use AI to manage supply chains, inventory, and logistics more effectively.

2.2.2 Enhanced Decision-Making

- **Predictive Analytics:** Leverage AI to forecast trends, customer behavior, and market dynamics.
- **Real-Time Insights:** Make informed decisions based on up-to-date data analysis.

2.2.3 Customer Engagement

- **Personalization:** Offer tailored products and services using AI-driven customer insights.
- **Improved Support:** Implement chatbots and virtual assistants to provide instant customer service.

2.3 Assessing Return on Investment (ROI)

Evaluating the potential ROI is crucial for securing stakeholder buy-in and allocating resources effectively.

2.3.1 Calculating Costs and Benefits

- **Initial Investment:** Hardware, software, and talent acquisition costs.
- **Operational Savings:** Reduced labor costs, increased productivity, and lower error rates.
- **Revenue Growth:** New product offerings, market penetration, and customer retention.

2.3.2 Risk Analysis

- **Technical Risks:** Potential implementation challenges and system failures.
- **Market Risks:** Uncertain customer acceptance and competitive responses.
- **Regulatory Risks:** Compliance with laws and regulations.

2.4 Building a Compelling Business Case

A well-crafted business case articulates the value proposition of AI initiatives.

2.4.1 Key Components

- **Executive Summary:** Concise overview of the AI project and its expected impact.
- **Problem Statement:** Clear definition of the issues the AI solution will address.
- **Solution Description:** Detailed explanation of the proposed AI application.
- **Financial Projections:** ROI calculations, cost-benefit analysis, and funding requirements.
- **Implementation Plan:** Timeline, milestones, and resource allocation.
- **Risk Management Plan:** Strategies for mitigating identified risks.

2.4.2 Gaining Stakeholder Support

- **Engage Early:** Involve key stakeholders from the project's inception.
- **Demonstrate Value:** Use pilot projects or prototypes to showcase potential benefits.
- **Address Concerns:** Be prepared to discuss challenges and how they will be managed.

2.5 Overcoming Barriers to AI Adoption

Implementing AI is not without obstacles. Recognizing and addressing these barriers is essential.

2.5.1 Organizational Resistance

- **Change Management:** Develop strategies to manage the human aspect of technological change.
- **Communication:** Maintain open lines of communication to alleviate fears and misconceptions.
- **Training and Development:** Invest in upskilling employees to work alongside AI systems.

2.5.2 Resource Constraints

- **Budget Limitations:** Explore cost-effective solutions like cloud-based AI services.
- **Talent Shortage:** Consider partnerships or outsourcing to access specialized skills.

2.5.3 Data Challenges

- **Data Quality:** Implement data governance practices to ensure accuracy and reliability.
- **Data Silos:** Integrate data across departments for a holistic AI approach.

2.6 Legal and Ethical Considerations

Navigating the legal and ethical landscape is critical for sustainable AI implementation.

2.6.1 Regulatory Compliance

- **Data Protection Laws:** Adhere to regulations like GDPR and CCPA regarding personal data.
- **Industry Regulations:** Comply with sector-specific guidelines, such as HIPAA in healthcare.

2.6.2 Ethical AI Practices

- **Bias and Fairness:** Ensure AI models do not perpetuate discrimination.
- **Transparency:** Maintain clear explanations of how AI systems make decisions.
- **Accountability:** Establish protocols for responsibility in case of AI-related issues.

2.7 Measuring Success

Defining clear metrics to evaluate the performance of AI initiatives ensures they deliver the intended value.

2.7.1 Key Performance Indicators (KPIs)

- **Operational Metrics:** Efficiency gains, error rate reductions, cost savings.
- **Financial Metrics:** ROI, revenue growth, profit margins.

- **Customer Metrics:** Satisfaction scores, retention rates, engagement levels.

2.7.2 Continuous Improvement

- **Feedback Loops:** Collect data to refine AI models and processes.
- **Benchmarking:** Compare performance against industry standards and best practices.

2.8 Case Study: AI Enhancing Customer Experience in Retail

2.8.1 Background

A leading retail chain sought to improve its customer experience to increase sales and loyalty.

2.8.2 Implementation

- **Personalized Recommendations:** Deployed AI algorithms to analyze customer behavior and suggest products.
- **Inventory Management:** Used predictive analytics to ensure product availability.
- **Chatbots:** Provided instant customer support across online platforms.

2.8.3 Results

- **Increased Sales:** Achieved a 15% rise in average transaction value.

- **Improved Customer Satisfaction:** Customer feedback indicated a higher level of satisfaction.
- **Operational Efficiency:** Reduced stockouts by 20%, leading to better inventory turnover.

Chapter 3: AI Applications Across Industries

Transforming Business Landscapes Through AI

3.1 Introduction to Industry-Specific AI Applications

Artificial Intelligence (AI) is reshaping industries by introducing new ways to solve complex problems, enhance efficiency, and create innovative products and services. This chapter explores how AI is being applied across various sectors, highlighting real-world examples and their impact.

3.2 Healthcare

3.2.1 Diagnostics and Medical Imaging

AI algorithms analyze medical images to detect anomalies such as tumors, fractures, or diseases.

- **Improved Accuracy:** AI can identify patterns that may be missed by human practitioners.
- **Faster Results:** Reduces the time needed to interpret complex images.

3.2.2 Personalized Medicine

AI processes patient data to tailor treatments based on individual genetic profiles and medical histories.

- **Predictive Analytics:** Forecasts patient responses to medications.
- **Enhanced Outcomes:** Increases the effectiveness of treatments.

3.2.3 Administrative Efficiency

Automating administrative tasks allows healthcare providers to focus more on patient care.

- **Scheduling Systems:** AI optimizes appointment scheduling to reduce wait times.
- **Electronic Health Records (EHR):** AI assists in maintaining and updating patient records accurately.

Case Study: AI in Early Disease Detection

A hospital implemented an AI system to analyze patient data and identify early signs of sepsis. The system reduced mortality rates by 20% by enabling prompt intervention.

3.3 Finance and Banking

3.3.1 Fraud Detection

AI monitors transactions in real-time to identify suspicious activities.

- **Anomaly Detection:** Flags deviations from normal behavior patterns.
- **Adaptive Learning:** Continuously improves detection as fraud tactics evolve.

3.3.2 Algorithmic Trading

AI systems execute trades based on market data analysis.

- **Speed and Efficiency:** Executes trades faster than humanly possible.
- **Data-Driven Decisions:** Minimizes emotional biases in trading.

3.3.3 Customer Service and Support

AI-powered chatbots handle customer inquiries efficiently.

- **24/7 Availability:** Provides support outside of regular business hours.
- **Personalized Interactions:** Uses customer data to tailor responses.

Case Study: AI Enhancing Credit Scoring

A fintech company used AI to analyze alternative data sources for credit scoring, expanding access to loans for underserved populations while maintaining low default rates.

3.4 Retail and E-Commerce

3.4.1 Inventory Optimization

AI predicts demand to manage stock levels effectively.

- **Reduced Overstock:** Minimizes excess inventory.
- **Prevent Stockouts:** Ensures popular items remain available.

3.4.2 Dynamic Pricing

Adjusts prices in real-time based on demand, competition, and other factors.

- **Maximized Revenue:** Optimizes pricing strategies for profitability.
- **Competitive Edge:** Responds quickly to market changes.

3.4.3 Visual Search

Allows customers to search for products using images.

- **Enhanced User Experience:** Simplifies the search process.
- **Increased Engagement:** Encourages exploration of product offerings.

Case Study: AI Driving Sales Growth

An online retailer implemented AI recommendation engines, resulting in a 35% increase in sales from personalized suggestions.

3.5 Manufacturing

3.5.1 Predictive Maintenance

AI analyzes data from sensors to predict equipment failures.

- **Reduced Downtime:** Schedules maintenance before breakdowns occur.
- **Cost Savings:** Lowers repair expenses and prolongs equipment life.

3.5.2 Quality Control

Automates inspection processes to detect defects.

- **Consistent Standards:** Maintains product quality uniformly.
- **Efficiency Gains:** Increases the speed of quality checks.

3.5.3 Supply Chain Management

Optimizes logistics and supplier relationships.

- **Demand Forecasting:** Aligns production with market needs.
- **Risk Management:** Identifies potential supply chain disruptions.

Case Study: AI Enhancing Production Efficiency

A manufacturing firm used AI to optimize its assembly line, achieving a 20% increase in productivity and a 15% reduction in waste.

3.6 Transportation and Logistics

3.6.1 Route Optimization

AI calculates the most efficient routes for deliveries.

- **Fuel Savings:** Reduces transportation costs.
- **Improved Delivery Times:** Enhances customer satisfaction.

3.6.2 Autonomous Vehicles

Development of self-driving cars and trucks.

- **Safety Improvements:** Reduces accidents caused by human error.
- **Labor Efficiency:** Addresses driver shortages.

3.6.3 Demand Forecasting

Predicts shipping volumes to allocate resources appropriately.

- **Resource Allocation:** Adjusts fleet size and staffing levels.
- **Customer Service:** Improves reliability of delivery schedules.

Case Study: AI Streamlining Logistics Operations

A global shipping company implemented AI for route planning, resulting in a 10% reduction in fuel consumption and faster delivery times.

3.7 Energy and Utilities

3.7.1 Smart Grids and Energy Management

AI optimizes energy distribution and consumption.

- **Load Balancing:** Adjusts supply based on demand patterns.
- **Renewable Integration:** Manages variability in renewable energy sources.

3.7.2 Predictive Maintenance

Monitors infrastructure to prevent outages.

- **Grid Reliability:** Reduces the frequency and duration of power outages.
- **Cost Efficiency:** Lowers maintenance expenses.

3.7.3 Consumer Energy Management

AI assists consumers in reducing energy usage.

- **Smart Thermostats:** Adjust settings based on occupancy and preferences.
- **Usage Insights:** Provides data on consumption patterns.

Case Study: AI Improving Energy Efficiency

An energy provider used AI to analyze consumption data, helping customers reduce usage by 15% through personalized recommendations.

3.8 Agriculture

3.8.1 Precision Farming

AI guides planting, harvesting, and resource application.

- **Yield Optimization:** Maximizes crop output.

- **Resource Conservation:** Minimizes water and fertilizer use.

3.8.2 Pest and Disease Detection

Identifies threats early to prevent crop damage.

- **Image Analysis:** Uses drones and sensors to monitor fields.
- **Timely Intervention:** Allows for quick response to issues.

3.8.3 Supply Chain Optimization

Manages the distribution of agricultural products.

- **Demand Forecasting:** Aligns production with market needs.
- **Waste Reduction:** Improves storage and transportation efficiency.

Case Study: AI Boosting Agricultural Productivity

A farm implemented AI for soil analysis and irrigation control, increasing yields by 10% while reducing water usage by 20%.

3.9 Telecommunications

3.9.1 Network Optimization

AI enhances network performance and reliability.

- **Traffic Management:** Allocates bandwidth efficiently.

- **Fault Prediction:** Anticipates network issues before they impact users.

3.9.2 Customer Analytics

Analyzes user data to improve services.

- **Churn Prediction:** Identifies customers at risk of leaving.
- **Personalized Offers:** Tailors promotions to individual needs.

3.9.3 Virtual Assistants

Automates customer support interactions.

- **Quick Resolution:** Addresses common issues without human intervention.
- **Cost Reduction:** Lowers support center expenses.

Case Study: AI Enhancing Network Performance

A telecom operator used AI to manage network congestion, improving average data speeds by 15% during peak hours.

3.10 Professional Services

3.10.1 Legal Sector

AI automates routine legal tasks.

- **Document Review:** Speeds up contract analysis and due diligence.

- **Legal Research:** Retrieves relevant case law efficiently.

3.10.2 Accounting and Finance

Streamlines financial processes.

- **Automated Bookkeeping:** Reduces errors in financial records.
- **Financial Analysis:** Provides real-time insights into financial performance.

3.10.3 Human Resources

Enhances recruitment and employee management.

- **Talent Acquisition:** Uses AI to screen candidates effectively.
- **Employee Engagement:** Analyzes feedback to improve workplace satisfaction.

Case Study: AI in Legal Services

A law firm implemented AI for contract review, reducing the time spent on document analysis by 40% and increasing accuracy.

Chapter 4: Developing an AI Strategy

Integrating Artificial Intelligence into Your Business Plan

4.1 Introduction to AI Strategy Development

An AI strategy outlines how an organization will use artificial intelligence to achieve its business objectives. It serves as a roadmap for integrating AI technologies into operations, products, and services.

4.1.1 Importance of a Well-Defined Strategy

- **Alignment with Goals:** Ensures AI initiatives support overall business objectives.
- **Resource Optimization:** Guides efficient allocation of time, budget, and personnel.
- **Risk Mitigation:** Identifies potential challenges and how to address them.

4.2 Assessing Organizational Readiness

Before implementing AI, evaluate your organization's preparedness.

4.2.1 Internal Capabilities

- **Technical Infrastructure:** Assess current technology and scalability.
- **Data Assets:** Evaluate data quality, availability, and management practices.
- **Talent Pool:** Identify skills gaps in AI, data science, and related areas.

4.2.2 Cultural Factors

- **Innovation Culture:** Gauge openness to change and experimentation.
- **Leadership Support:** Ensure executive backing for AI initiatives.
- **Employee Engagement:** Involve staff in planning to foster buy-in.

4.3 Setting Clear Objectives

Define what you aim to achieve with AI.

4.3.1 Business Goals

- **Efficiency Improvement:** Automate processes to reduce costs.
- **Revenue Growth:** Develop new products or services.
- **Customer Satisfaction:** Enhance user experiences.

4.3.2 Key Performance Indicators (KPIs)

- **Measurable Targets:** Establish specific metrics to track progress.
- **Timeframes:** Set realistic deadlines for achieving objectives.

4.4 Identifying Use Cases

Select AI applications that offer the highest value.

4.4.1 Prioritization Criteria

- **Impact Potential:** Estimate the benefits to the organization.
- **Feasibility:** Consider technical complexity and resource requirements.
- **Alignment:** Ensure use cases support strategic goals.

4.4.2 Examples of Use Cases

- **Predictive Maintenance:** For manufacturing or equipment-heavy industries.
- **Customer Segmentation:** In marketing and sales.
- **Risk Assessment:** In finance and insurance.

4.5 Building a Cross-Functional Team

Assemble a team with diverse expertise to drive AI projects.

4.5.1 Team Composition

- **Data Scientists:** Develop AI models and algorithms.

- **Domain Experts:** Provide industry-specific knowledge.
- **IT Professionals:** Manage infrastructure and integration.
- **Project Managers:** Coordinate activities and timelines.

4.5.2 Collaboration Practices

- **Regular Communication:** Hold meetings to align on objectives and progress.
- **Knowledge Sharing:** Encourage learning across disciplines.
- **Stakeholder Engagement:** Involve key stakeholders throughout the project.

4.6 Choosing the Right Technologies

Select AI tools and platforms that meet your needs.

4.6.1 Build vs. Buy Decision

- **In-House Development:** Offers customization but requires significant resources.
- **Off-the-Shelf Solutions:** Faster deployment with lower upfront costs.

4.6.2 Evaluation Criteria

- **Scalability:** Ability to grow with your business.
- **Compatibility:** Integration with existing systems.
- **Vendor Support:** Availability of technical assistance and updates.

4.7 Data Strategy and Management

Develop a robust data strategy to support AI initiatives.

4.7.1 Data Governance

- **Policies and Procedures:** Establish rules for data usage and management.
- **Compliance:** Ensure adherence to legal and regulatory requirements.

4.7.2 Data Infrastructure

- **Storage Solutions:** Implement databases and data lakes as needed.
- **Data Integration:** Consolidate data from various sources.

4.7.3 Data Quality Assurance

- **Data Cleansing:** Remove inaccuracies and inconsistencies.
- **Data Enrichment:** Enhance data with additional relevant information.

4.8 Implementation Roadmap

Create a step-by-step plan for deploying AI solutions.

4.8.1 Phased Approach

- **Pilot Projects:** Test AI applications on a small scale.

- **Scaling Up:** Expand successful pilots to wider operations.
- **Continuous Improvement:** Refine AI models based on feedback and results.

4.8.2 Timeline and Milestones

- **Short-Term Goals:** Achievable within months.
- **Long-Term Objectives:** Targets set for one year or more.

4.9 Risk Management

Identify and mitigate risks associated with AI implementation.

4.9.1 Common Risks

- **Technical Failures:** System outages or performance issues.
- **Data Breaches:** Unauthorized access to sensitive information.
- **Regulatory Changes:** New laws affecting AI use.

4.9.2 Mitigation Strategies

- **Robust Security Measures:** Implement strong cybersecurity protocols.
- **Compliance Monitoring:** Stay informed about regulatory developments.
- **Fallback Plans:** Prepare contingency measures for potential failures.

4.10 Change Management

Facilitate organizational adaptation to AI technologies.

4.10.1 Communication Strategy

- **Transparency:** Share information about AI projects openly.
- **Address Concerns:** Listen to employee feedback and address fears.

4.10.2 Training and Development

- **Skill Enhancement:** Offer training programs to upskill staff.
- **Role Redefinition:** Adjust job descriptions as necessary.

4.10.3 Cultural Integration

- **Innovation Encouragement:** Promote experimentation and learning.
- **Recognition Programs:** Acknowledge contributions to AI initiatives.

4.11 Monitoring and Evaluation

Track the performance of AI implementations to ensure they meet objectives.

4.11.1 Performance Tracking

- **Regular Reporting:** Generate reports on KPIs.

- **Dashboards:** Use visualization tools for real-time monitoring.

4.11.2 Feedback Loops

- **User Feedback:** Collect input from employees and customers.
- **Model Refinement:** Update AI models based on new data and insights.

4.12 Case Study: Crafting an AI Strategy for a Financial Institution

4.12.1 Background

A mid-sized bank aimed to enhance customer service and operational efficiency through AI.

4.12.2 Strategy Development

- **Assessment:** Evaluated current capabilities and identified data assets.
- **Objective Setting:** Targeted a 15% reduction in customer service response times.
- **Use Case Selection:** Chose to implement AI chatbots and fraud detection systems.

4.12.3 Implementation

- **Team Formation:** Created a cross-functional team including IT, customer service, and compliance.

- **Technology Selection:** Opted for a combination of in-house development and third-party solutions.
- **Change Management:** Conducted training sessions and maintained open communication.

4.12.4 Results

- **Improved Efficiency:** Reduced average response times by 20%.
- **Customer Satisfaction:** Increased satisfaction scores by 10%.
- **Operational Savings:** Achieved cost reductions in customer service operations.

Chapter 5: Implementing AI Solutions

From Planning to Execution

5.1 Introduction to AI Implementation

Transitioning from strategy to execution is a critical phase in leveraging Artificial Intelligence (AI) for business success. This chapter provides a step-by-step guide to implementing AI solutions, ensuring that projects are executed effectively and deliver the intended value.

5.1.1 Importance of a Structured Approach

- **Minimize Risks:** A systematic implementation reduces the likelihood of technical failures and resource wastage.
- **Ensure Alignment:** Keeps the project aligned with business objectives and stakeholder expectations.
- **Facilitate Adoption:** Enhances user acceptance and integration into existing processes.

5.2 Preparation and Planning

5.2.1 Define Clear Objectives and Scope

- **Specific Goals:** Outline what the AI solution aims to achieve.

- **Project Scope:** Determine the boundaries to prevent scope creep.
- **Success Criteria:** Establish measurable outcomes to assess performance.

5.2.2 Assemble the Implementation Team

- **Project Manager:** Oversees the project and coordinates between teams.
- **Data Scientists and Engineers:** Develop and deploy AI models.
- **IT Specialists:** Handle infrastructure and integration.
- **Business Analysts:** Ensure the solution meets business needs.
- **Change Management Lead:** Manages organizational transition.

5.2.3 Develop a Detailed Project Plan

- **Timeline:** Set milestones and deadlines.
- **Resource Allocation:** Assign tasks and responsibilities.
- **Budgeting:** Outline financial requirements and controls.
- **Risk Management Plan:** Identify potential obstacles and mitigation strategies.

5.3 Data Preparation

5.3.1 Data Collection

- **Identify Data Sources:** Determine internal and external sources of relevant data.
- **Data Accessibility:** Ensure data can be retrieved efficiently.
- **Permission and Compliance:** Verify that data usage complies with legal and regulatory standards.

5.3.2 Data Cleaning and Preprocessing

- **Data Quality Assessment:** Check for inaccuracies, inconsistencies, and missing values.
- **Data Transformation:** Normalize and format data for analysis.
- **Feature Selection:** Choose relevant variables that influence model performance.

5.3.3 Data Augmentation (if necessary)

- **Synthetic Data Generation:** Create additional data using simulations or algorithms.
- **Data Enrichment:** Incorporate supplementary data to enhance model inputs.

5.4 Model Development

5.4.1 Selecting the Appropriate Algorithm

- **Problem Type:** Classification, regression, clustering, etc.
- **Data Characteristics:** Structured vs. unstructured data.
- **Performance Requirements:** Accuracy, speed, scalability.

5.4.2 Training the Model

- **Training Set:** Use a portion of the data to teach the model.
- **Validation Set:** Monitor the model's performance during training.
- **Hyperparameter Tuning:** Adjust parameters to optimize results.

5.4.3 Testing and Evaluation

- **Test Set:** Evaluate the model on unseen data to assess generalization.
- **Performance Metrics:** Accuracy, precision, recall, F1 score, etc.
- **Error Analysis:** Identify and address areas where the model underperforms.

5.5 Deployment

5.5.1 Infrastructure Setup

- **Hardware Requirements:** Servers, GPUs, cloud services.
- **Software Environment:** Necessary libraries, frameworks, and operating systems.
- **Scalability Considerations:** Ability to handle increased load.

5.5.2 Integration with Existing Systems

- **APIs and Interfaces:** Connect the AI solution with current applications.
- **Data Pipelines:** Ensure seamless data flow between systems.
- **Security Measures:** Protect against unauthorized access and data breaches.

5.5.3 User Interface Design

- **Usability:** Create an intuitive interface for end-users.
- **Accessibility:** Ensure the solution is accessible to all users, including those with disabilities.
- **Feedback Mechanisms:** Allow users to report issues or provide suggestions.

5.6 Monitoring and Maintenance

5.6.1 Performance Monitoring

- **Real-Time Analytics:** Track the AI system's performance continuously.
- **Alert Systems:** Notify stakeholders of anomalies or failures.
- **Logging:** Record system activities for analysis and troubleshooting.

5.6.2 Model Retraining and Updates

- **Drift Detection:** Identify when the model's performance degrades over time.
- **Continuous Learning:** Update the model with new data to maintain accuracy.
- **Version Control:** Manage changes to the model and deployment.

5.6.3 Technical Support and Troubleshooting

- **Support Team:** Establish a team to handle issues promptly.
- **Documentation:** Maintain comprehensive guides and FAQs.
- **User Training:** Educate users on new features or changes.

5.7 Change Management in Implementation

5.7.1 Communication Strategy

- **Stakeholder Updates:** Regularly inform stakeholders about progress.
- **Transparency:** Share successes and challenges openly.
- **Messaging:** Tailor communication to different audience segments.

5.7.2 Training and User Adoption

- **Training Programs:** Provide hands-on training sessions.
- **Learning Resources:** Create manuals, tutorials, and e-learning modules.
- **Incentives:** Encourage adoption through recognition or rewards.

5.7.3 Addressing Resistance

- **Feedback Channels:** Allow employees to voice concerns.
- **Support Structures:** Offer assistance to those struggling with the transition.
- **Cultural Integration:** Promote a culture that embraces innovation.

5.8 Legal and Ethical Compliance

5.8.1 Data Privacy

- **Regulatory Adherence:** Comply with GDPR, CCPA, and other relevant laws.
- **Consent Management:** Obtain and manage user consent where necessary.
- **Anonymization:** Remove personally identifiable information when appropriate.

5.8.2 Ethical AI Practices

- **Bias Mitigation:** Ensure the model does not perpetuate unfair biases.
- **Transparency:** Maintain explainability in how the AI makes decisions.
- **Accountability:** Establish protocols for addressing errors or harm caused by AI.

5.9 Case Study: Implementing an AI-Powered Customer Support System

5.9.1 Background

A telecommunications company aimed to improve customer service efficiency by implementing an AI chatbot to handle routine inquiries.

5.9.2 Implementation Steps

1. **Objective Definition:** Reduce average response time and improve customer satisfaction.
2. **Team Assembly:** Included AI specialists, IT staff, customer service representatives, and a project manager.
3. **Data Preparation:** Collected historical customer interactions to train the chatbot.
4. **Model Development:** Used natural language processing (NLP) algorithms to understand and respond to customer queries.
5. **Deployment:** Integrated the chatbot into the company's website and mobile app.
6. **Monitoring:** Set up dashboards to track usage, response times, and customer feedback.
7. **Change Management:** Trained customer service staff to work alongside the chatbot and handle escalated issues.

5.9.3 Results

- **Efficiency Gains:** Handled 50% of customer inquiries without human intervention.
- **Customer Satisfaction:** Improved satisfaction scores by 15%.
- **Cost Savings:** Reduced operational costs by decreasing the workload on human agents.

Chapter 6: Managing Change and Cultivating an AI-Ready Culture

Embracing Transformation within the Organization

6.1 Introduction to Organizational Change Management

The successful integration of AI technologies goes beyond technical implementation; it necessitates a shift in organizational culture and mindset. This chapter explores strategies for managing change and fostering a culture that is receptive to AI.

6.1.1 The Human Element in AI Adoption

- **Employee Acceptance:** Crucial for smooth transition and utilization of AI systems.
- **Cultural Alignment:** Ensures that AI initiatives resonate with organizational values and practices.

6.2 Understanding the Impact of AI on the Workforce

6.2.1 Job Transformation

- **Automation of Routine Tasks:** AI takes over repetitive tasks, altering job responsibilities.
- **Emergence of New Roles:** Creates demand for new skills and positions, such as AI ethics officers or data analysts.

6.2.2 Employee Concerns

- **Job Security:** Fear of redundancy due to automation.
- **Skill Relevance:** Anxiety over outdated skills and the need for reskilling.
- **Change Fatigue:** Resistance due to constant organizational changes.

6.3 Strategies for Effective Change Management

6.3.1 Leadership and Vision

- **Executive Sponsorship:** Leaders must champion AI initiatives.
- **Clear Vision:** Articulate how AI aligns with the organization's future.

6.3.2 Communication Plan

- **Transparent Messaging:** Share the purpose, benefits, and impacts of AI projects.
- **Two-Way Dialogue:** Encourage feedback and address concerns promptly.
- **Consistent Updates:** Provide regular progress reports.

6.3.3 Employee Involvement

- **Inclusive Approach:** Involve employees in planning and implementation.
- **Empowerment:** Give staff ownership over aspects of the AI transition.
- **Recognition:** Acknowledge contributions and successes.

6.4 Building an AI-Ready Culture

6.4.1 Promoting a Growth Mindset

- **Encourage Learning:** Foster an environment where continuous learning is valued.
- **Accepting Failure:** View setbacks as opportunities for improvement.

6.4.2 Skill Development and Training

- **Reskilling Programs:** Offer training to develop new competencies.
- **Learning Platforms:** Provide access to online courses, workshops, and seminars.

- **Mentorship:** Pair employees with experts for guidance.

6.4.3 Fostering Collaboration

- **Cross-Functional Teams:** Encourage collaboration between departments.
- **Knowledge Sharing:** Create forums for exchanging ideas and best practices.
- **Innovation Labs:** Establish spaces dedicated to experimentation and innovation.

6.5 Addressing Ethical and Social Considerations

6.5.1 Ethical AI Use

- **Ethics Committees:** Form groups to oversee AI ethics.
- **Guidelines and Policies:** Develop codes of conduct for AI development and use.

6.5.2 Diversity and Inclusion

- **Bias Mitigation:** Ensure AI does not perpetuate discrimination.
- **Inclusive Teams:** Build diverse teams to bring varied perspectives.

6.6 Measuring Cultural Change

6.6.1 Key Indicators

- **Engagement Levels:** Monitor participation in AI initiatives.
- **Employee Feedback:** Use surveys and interviews to gauge sentiment.
- **Adoption Rates:** Track usage of AI tools and processes.

6.6.2 Adjusting Strategies

- **Responsive Action:** Modify approaches based on feedback and outcomes.
- **Celebrate Milestones:** Recognize progress to maintain momentum.

6.7 Case Study: Cultivating an AI-Ready Culture in a Manufacturing Company

6.7.1 Background

A manufacturing firm sought to integrate AI into its operations but faced resistance from employees concerned about job security.

6.7.2 Change Management Actions

1. **Leadership Engagement:** Executives communicated the vision and addressed concerns.

2. **Transparent Communication:** Held town hall meetings to explain the AI strategy.
3. **Employee Involvement:** Formed committees including employees to guide AI projects.
4. **Training Programs:** Provided reskilling opportunities for affected workers.
5. **Ethical Framework:** Established guidelines to ensure responsible AI use.

6.7.3 Outcomes

- **Improved Morale:** Employees felt valued and part of the transformation.
- **Successful Implementation:** High adoption rates of new AI systems.
- **Enhanced Productivity:** Achieved efficiency gains without significant job losses.

Chapter 7: Measuring Success and Ensuring Continuous Improvement

Evaluating the Impact of AI Initiatives

7.1 Importance of Measurement and Evaluation

Assessing the performance of AI initiatives is critical to understanding their value and guiding future efforts. This chapter outlines methods for measuring success and promoting continuous improvement.

7.1.1 Aligning Metrics with Objectives

- **Strategic Alignment:** Ensure that evaluation metrics reflect business goals.
- **Holistic Assessment:** Consider both quantitative and qualitative outcomes.

7.2 Defining Key Performance Indicators (KPIs)

7.2.1 Operational Metrics

- **Efficiency Gains:** Time saved, increased throughput.

- **Cost Reductions:** Savings from automation and optimization.
- **Error Rates:** Reduction in mistakes or defects.

7.2.2 Financial Metrics

- **Return on Investment (ROI):** Financial returns relative to the investment made.
- **Revenue Growth:** Increases attributable to AI-driven products or services.
- **Profit Margins:** Improvement due to cost efficiencies.

7.2.3 Customer-Focused Metrics

- **Satisfaction Scores:** Customer feedback and ratings.
- **Retention Rates:** Loyalty improvements resulting from better service.
- **Engagement Levels:** Interaction frequency and depth.

7.2.4 Employee Metrics

- **Adoption Rates:** Usage levels of AI tools among staff.
- **Productivity Measures:** Output per employee.
- **Training Participation:** Engagement in skill development programs.

7.3 Data Collection and Analysis

7.3.1 Establishing Baselines

- **Pre-Implementation Data:** Collect metrics before AI deployment to compare against post-implementation results.

7.3.2 Ongoing Monitoring

- **Real-Time Dashboards:** Visualize data for immediate insights.
- **Regular Reporting:** Schedule periodic reviews to assess progress.

7.3.3 Advanced Analytics

- **Data Mining:** Extract patterns and trends.
- **Predictive Analytics:** Forecast future performance based on current data.

7.4 Evaluating AI Model Performance

7.4.1 Technical Metrics

- **Accuracy:** Correct predictions or classifications.
- **Precision and Recall:** Balance between identifying true positives and minimizing false positives.
- **F1 Score:** Harmonizes precision and recall into a single metric.

7.4.2 Model Robustness

- **Generalization:** Model's ability to perform on unseen data.
- **Scalability:** Performance under increased load or data volume.
- **Resilience:** Ability to handle data anomalies or adversarial inputs.

7.5 Ensuring Compliance and Ethical Standards

7.5.1 Regulatory Compliance

- **Audit Trails:** Maintain records to demonstrate adherence to laws.
- **Data Privacy Checks:** Regularly verify compliance with data protection standards.

7.5.2 Ethical Evaluations

- **Bias Assessments:** Test models for discriminatory outcomes.
- **Transparency Reviews:** Ensure explanations of AI decisions are accessible.

7.6 Continuous Improvement Processes

7.6.1 Feedback Loops

- **User Feedback:** Collect input from employees and customers using AI systems.

- **Performance Reviews:** Regularly assess outcomes against goals.

7.6.2 Iterative Development

- **Agile Methodologies:** Adopt flexible approaches for quick adjustments.
- **Model Retraining:** Update AI models with new data and insights.

7.6.3 Benchmarking

- **Industry Standards:** Compare performance against peers.
- **Best Practices:** Incorporate proven strategies and techniques.

7.7 Scaling Successful AI Initiatives

7.7.1 Identifying Scalable Solutions

- **Resource Availability:** Ensure necessary infrastructure and talent.
- **Process Standardization:** Develop repeatable processes.

7.7.2 Managing Risks in Scaling

- **Capacity Planning:** Anticipate resource needs.
- **Quality Control:** Maintain performance standards during expansion.

7.7.3 Replicating Success

- **Documentation:** Record methodologies and lessons learned.
- **Knowledge Transfer:** Share expertise across the organization.

7.8 Case Study: Measuring Success in an AI-Driven Marketing Campaign

7.8.1 Background

A retail company implemented AI to personalize marketing efforts, aiming to increase customer engagement and sales.

7.8.2 Evaluation Metrics

- **Engagement Rates:** Monitored click-through and open rates.
- **Conversion Rates:** Tracked purchases resulting from marketing efforts.
- **Average Order Value:** Measured changes in spending per transaction.
- **Customer Lifetime Value (CLV):** Assessed the long-term value of customers.

7.8.3 Results and Analysis

- **Increased Engagement:** Click-through rates improved by 25%.
- **Higher Conversions:** Conversion rates rose by 15%.

- **Revenue Growth:** Average order value increased by 10%, boosting overall sales.
- **Enhanced CLV:** Projected long-term value of customers improved due to increased loyalty.

7.8.4 Continuous Improvement Actions

- **Model Refinement:** Adjusted algorithms based on performance data.
- **Expanded Use Cases:** Applied successful strategies to other marketing channels.
- **Feedback Integration:** Incorporated customer feedback to enhance personalization.

Chapter 8: The Future of AI in Business

Preparing for Emerging Trends and Technologies

8.1 Introduction to Emerging AI Trends

As AI continues to evolve, businesses must stay informed about emerging trends to remain competitive. This chapter explores future developments in AI and how organizations can prepare.

8.1.1 The Accelerating Pace of Change

- **Technological Advancements:** Rapid improvements in computational power, algorithms, and data availability.
- **Global Adoption:** Increasing AI integration across industries and geographies.

8.2 Key Emerging Technologies in AI

8.2.1 Edge Computing

- **Definition:** Processing data near the source (devices, sensors) rather than centralized servers.
- **Benefits:** Reduced latency, enhanced privacy, and lower bandwidth usage.

- **Applications:** Real-time analytics in IoT devices, autonomous vehicles, and industrial automation.

8.2.2 Explainable AI (XAI)

- **Definition:** AI systems designed to provide clear explanations of their decisions.
- **Importance:** Enhances trust, facilitates regulatory compliance, and aids in debugging.
- **Applications:** High-stakes industries like healthcare, finance, and legal services.

8.2.3 AI and Quantum Computing

- **Potential Impact:** Quantum computers could solve complex problems beyond classical computing capabilities.
- **Applications:** Optimization problems, cryptography, and advanced simulations.

8.2.4 Human-AI Collaboration

- **Augmented Intelligence:** AI systems that enhance human decision-making rather than replace it.
- **Applications:** Decision support systems, creative industries, and complex problem-solving.

8.3 Societal and Ethical Considerations

8.3.1 AI Governance

- **Frameworks and Standards:** Development of guidelines for responsible AI use.
- **Global Collaboration:** International efforts to harmonize regulations and best practices.

8.3.2 Workforce Evolution

- **Job Transformation:** Emphasis on roles requiring creativity, empathy, and complex reasoning.
- **Lifelong Learning:** Necessity for continuous skill development.

8.3.3 Data Privacy and Security

- **Advanced Threats:** AI-powered cyberattacks necessitate stronger defenses.
- **Privacy Preservation Techniques:** Federated learning, differential privacy.

8.4 Preparing for the Future

8.4.1 Strategic Foresight

- **Trend Analysis:** Monitor technological and market developments.
- **Scenario Planning:** Anticipate various future states to inform strategy.

8.4.2 Investment in Innovation

- **Research and Development:** Allocate resources to explore new AI technologies.
- **Partnerships:** Collaborate with startups, academia, and research institutions.

8.4.3 Agile Organizational Structures

- **Flexibility:** Adapt quickly to changes and new opportunities.
- **Empowered Teams:** Decentralize decision-making to enhance responsiveness.

8.5 Case Study: Embracing Future AI Trends in a Tech Company

8.5.1 Background

A technology firm recognized the need to stay ahead in AI innovation to maintain its market position.

8.5.2 Actions Taken

1. **Innovation Lab Creation:** Established a dedicated team to explore emerging AI technologies.
2. **Investment in Edge Computing:** Developed solutions for IoT devices requiring real-time processing.
3. **Focus on Explainable AI:** Integrated XAI principles into product development.
4. **Ethical AI Framework:** Implemented policies to guide responsible AI practices.

5. **Talent Development:** Launched programs for continuous learning and skill enhancement.

8.5.3 Outcomes

- **Product Differentiation:** Introduced cutting-edge offerings that set them apart from competitors.
- **Market Leadership:** Positioned as an industry thought leader in AI innovation.
- **Sustainable Growth:** Achieved consistent revenue growth through innovation-driven strategies.

Chapter 9: Resources and Tools for AI Implementation

Leveraging Platforms, Frameworks, and Services to Accelerate AI Adoption

---

9.1 Introduction to AI Resources and Tools

Implementing Artificial Intelligence (AI) solutions requires access to various resources, including software tools, platforms, and services that facilitate development, deployment, and management. This chapter explores essential resources and tools that businesses can utilize to accelerate their AI initiatives.

9.1.1 Importance of the Right Tools

- **Efficiency:** Streamline development processes.
- **Scalability:** Support growth and increased demand.
- **Cost-Effectiveness:** Optimize resource utilization and reduce expenses.

9.2 AI Development Platforms

9.2.1 Cloud-Based Platforms

- **Amazon Web Services (AWS) AI Services**

- Offers machine learning services like Amazon SageMaker.
- Provides scalable infrastructure and tools for developers.
- **Microsoft Azure AI**
  - Includes Azure Machine Learning and Cognitive Services.
  - Integrates with other Azure services for seamless deployment.
- **Google Cloud AI Platform**
  - Features tools like AutoML and TensorFlow Enterprise.
  - Emphasizes ease of use and integration with Google services.

9.2.2 On-Premises Solutions

- **IBM Watson**
  - Provides AI capabilities for businesses needing on-premises solutions.
  - Focuses on natural language processing and data analytics.
- **Open-Source Platforms**
  - **TensorFlow:** An open-source library for machine learning.
  - **PyTorch:** A framework favored for deep learning applications.

9.3 AI Frameworks and Libraries

9.3.1 Machine Learning Libraries

- **Scikit-Learn**
  - Ideal for data mining and data analysis.
  - Supports classification, regression, and clustering algorithms.
- **XGBoost**
  - Optimized for gradient boosting decision trees.
  - Known for performance and speed.

9.3.2 Deep Learning Frameworks

- **TensorFlow**
  - Developed by Google Brain Team.
  - Widely used for neural network development.
- **PyTorch**
  - Developed by Facebook's AI Research lab.
  - Preferred for dynamic computational graphs.

9.3.3 Natural Language Processing (NLP) Tools

- **NLTK (Natural Language Toolkit)**
  - A suite of libraries for symbolic and statistical NLP.
- **spaCy**
  - Industrial-strength NLP library for advanced processing.

9.4 Data Management Tools

9.4.1 Data Integration and ETL

- **Apache Kafka**
  - Real-time data streaming platform.
- **Talend**
  - Provides data integration and management solutions.

9.4.2 Data Storage Solutions

- **Hadoop Distributed File System (HDFS)**
  - Handles large data sets across multiple machines.
- **NoSQL Databases**
  - **MongoDB:** Document-oriented database for unstructured data.
  - **Cassandra:** Highly scalable and available database.

9.4.3 Data Visualization Tools

- **Tableau**
  - Creates interactive visual analytics.
- **Power BI**
  - Microsoft's business analytics service.

9.5 AI as a Service (AIaaS)

9.5.1 Overview of AIaaS

- Provides ready-made AI services that can be integrated into applications.
- Reduces the need for in-house AI expertise.

9.5.2 Examples of AIaaS Providers

- **IBM Watson Assistant**
  - Enables the creation of conversational interfaces.
- **Google Cloud AutoML**
  - Allows custom machine learning models with minimal coding.
- **Microsoft Cognitive Services**
  - Offers APIs for vision, speech, language, and decision-making.

9.6 Ethical AI Tools

9.6.1 Bias Detection Tools

- **IBM AI Fairness 360**
  - An open-source toolkit to detect and mitigate bias.
- **Google What-If Tool**
  - Visualizes model behavior and analyzes fairness.

9.6.2 Explainability Tools

- **LIME (Local Interpretable Model-Agnostic Explanations)**
  - Explains predictions of any classifier in an interpretable manner.
- **SHAP (SHapley Additive exPlanations)**
  - Provides unified measurements of feature importance.

9.7 Collaboration and Project Management Tools

9.7.1 Version Control Systems

- **Git**
  - Tracks changes in source code during software development.
- **GitHub/GitLab**
  - Platforms for hosting and collaborating on Git repositories.

9.7.2 Project Management Software

- **JIRA**
  - Helps plan, track, and manage agile software development projects.
- **Asana/Trello**
  - Facilitates task management and team collaboration.

9.8 Training and Skill Development Resources

9.8.1 Online Learning Platforms

- **Coursera**
  - Offers courses and specializations from universities and companies.
- **edX**
  - Provides access to high-quality education from top institutions.

9.8.2 Certification Programs

- **Microsoft Certified: Azure AI Engineer Associate**
- **Google Cloud Certified - Professional Data Engineer**
- **IBM Data Science Professional Certificate**

9.9 Case Study: Utilizing AI Tools in a Startup Environment

9.9.1 Background

A tech startup aimed to develop an AI-driven analytics platform with limited resources.

9.9.2 Tools and Resources Used

- **Cloud Services:** Used AWS SageMaker for model development.
- **Open-Source Libraries:** Implemented models using TensorFlow and Scikit-Learn.

- **Data Storage:** Utilized MongoDB for handling unstructured data.
- **Collaboration:** Employed GitHub for version control and Slack for team communication.
- **Skill Development:** Team members took online courses on Coursera to enhance their AI expertise.

9.9.3 Outcomes

- **Rapid Development:** Accelerated product development timelines.
- **Cost Savings:** Reduced expenses by leveraging open-source tools.
- **Skill Enhancement:** Improved team capabilities through targeted training.

Chapter 10: Glossary of AI Terms

A Comprehensive Reference for Understanding AI Concepts

A

- **Algorithm:** A set of rules or instructions designed to perform a specific task.
- **Artificial Intelligence (AI):** The simulation of human intelligence processes by machines, especially computer systems.

B

- **Big Data:** Extremely large data sets that may be analyzed computationally to reveal patterns, trends, and associations.
- **Bias (in AI):** Systematic error introduced into data or algorithms leading to unfair outcomes.

C

- **Cloud Computing:** Delivery of computing services over the internet ("the cloud").
- **Clustering:** Unsupervised learning technique grouping similar data points together.

D

- **Data Mining:** The practice of examining large databases to generate new information.
- **Deep Learning:** A subset of machine learning involving neural networks with multiple layers.

E

- **Edge Computing:** Processing data near the data source to reduce latency.
- **Explainable AI (XAI):** AI systems that provide human-understandable explanations of their decisions.

F

- **Feature Engineering:** The process of selecting, modifying, or creating features to improve model performance.
- **Federated Learning:** Machine learning method that allows training on decentralized data.

G

- **Generative Adversarial Networks (GANs):** A class of machine learning frameworks where two networks compete to improve accuracy.

H

- **Hyperparameter:** A parameter whose value is set before the learning process begins.

I

- **Internet of Things (IoT):** Network of physical objects embedded with sensors and connectivity.
- **Inferencing:** The process of using a trained machine learning model to make predictions.

L

- **Machine Learning (ML):** A subset of AI that enables systems to learn from data.
- **Natural Language Processing (NLP):** AI subfield focused on the interaction between computers and human language.

O

- **Overfitting:** A modeling error where a function corresponds too closely to a particular set of data and may fail to fit additional data.

P

- **Predictive Analytics:** The practice of extracting information from existing data sets to forecast future probabilities.

- **Python:** A high-level programming language widely used in AI and machine learning.

R

- **Reinforcement Learning:** A type of machine learning where an agent learns to make decisions by taking actions that maximize cumulative reward.
- **Robotics:** The branch of technology dealing with the design and operation of robots.

S

- **Supervised Learning:** Machine learning task of learning a function that maps input to output based on example input-output pairs.
- **Scalability:** The capability of a system to handle a growing amount of work.

T

- **TensorFlow:** An open-source software library for machine learning.
- **Training Data:** Dataset used to train a model.

U

- **Unsupervised Learning:** Machine learning using data that is unlabeled and allowing the algorithm to act on that information without guidance.

V

- **Validation Data:** Data used to provide an unbiased evaluation of a model fit during training.
- **Virtual Assistant:** AI software agent that can perform tasks or services based on user commands.

W

- **Weights (in Neural Networks):** Parameters within the network that transform input data within the network's hidden layers.

Chapter 11: Further Reading and Learning Opportunities

Expanding Your Knowledge on AI and Its Applications

11.1 Foundational Books on AI

- **"Artificial Intelligence: A Modern Approach"** by Stuart Russell and Peter Norvig
  - Comprehensive textbook covering a broad range of AI topics.
- **"The Master Algorithm"** by Pedro Domingos
  - Explores the quest for a universal learner and the future of machine learning.
- **"Deep Learning"** by Ian Goodfellow, Yoshua Bengio, and Aaron Courville
  - An in-depth look at deep learning techniques and theories.

11.2 Industry-Specific AI Resources

Healthcare

- **"Artificial Intelligence in Healthcare"** by Adam Bohr and Kaveh Memarzadeh
  - Discusses AI applications in medical diagnostics, treatment, and patient care.

Finance

- **"AI in Finance"** by Yves Hilpisch
  - Explores how AI is transforming financial services and quantitative finance.

Marketing

- **"Artificial Intelligence for Marketing"** by Jim Sterne
  - Guides marketers on leveraging AI for customer engagement and analytics.

11.3 Online Courses and Certifications

Machine Learning

- **Machine Learning by Stanford University (Coursera)**
  - Taught by Andrew Ng, covers fundamental concepts.
- **Deep Learning Specialization (Coursera)**
  - Series of courses focusing on deep learning techniques.

AI Strategy

- **AI for Everyone (Coursera)**
  - Non-technical course designed to help understand AI's business implications.

Data Science

- **IBM Data Science Professional Certificate (Coursera)**
  - Comprehensive program covering data science tools and methodologies.

11.4 Research Papers and Journals

- **"Attention Is All You Need"** by Vaswani et al.
  - Introduces the Transformer model in NLP.
- **"ImageNet Classification with Deep Convolutional Neural Networks"** by Krizhevsky et al.
  - Landmark paper in image recognition using deep learning.

11.5 Conferences and Events

- **NeurIPS (Neural Information Processing Systems)**
  - Premier conference on AI and machine learning research.
- **AI Summit**
  - Focuses on AI applications in business and industry.

11.6 Professional Organizations

- **Association for the Advancement of Artificial Intelligence (AAAI)**
  - Promotes research and responsible use of AI.

- **International Machine Learning Society (IMLS)**
  - Supports machine learning research and conferences.

11.7 Online Communities and Forums

- **Stack Overflow**
  - Platform for asking and answering programming and development questions.
- **Reddit Communities**
  - Subreddits like r/MachineLearning and r/ArtificialIntelligence for discussions.

11.8 Podcasts and Videos

- **"Artificial Intelligence" Podcast by Lex Fridman**
  - Interviews with AI researchers and thought leaders.
- **TED Talks on AI**
  - Short talks covering various AI topics and perspectives.

Chapter 12: Conclusion

Embracing AI for a Competitive Future

12.1 Recap of Key Insights

Throughout this book, we've explored the multifaceted world of Artificial Intelligence and its profound impact on business. Key takeaways include:

- **Understanding AI Fundamentals:** Grasping what AI is and how machine learning and deep learning contribute to its capabilities.
- **Strategic Implementation:** Recognizing the importance of aligning AI initiatives with business objectives and developing a comprehensive strategy.
- **Industry Applications:** Learning how AI is transforming various sectors, offering opportunities for innovation and efficiency.
- **Change Management:** Emphasizing the human element in AI adoption, including managing cultural shifts and employee engagement.
- **Measuring Success:** Establishing metrics to evaluate AI initiatives and ensuring continuous improvement.
- **Preparing for the Future:** Staying informed about emerging trends and technologies to remain competitive.

12.2 The Imperative of Ethical AI

As AI becomes increasingly integrated into business operations, ethical considerations must remain at the forefront:

- **Fairness and Bias Mitigation:** Actively working to prevent discriminatory outcomes.
- **Transparency and Explainability:** Ensuring AI decisions can be understood and scrutinized.
- **Accountability:** Establishing clear responsibility for AI-driven actions.

12.3 The Road Ahead

The journey with AI is ongoing and dynamic:

- **Continuous Learning:** Encouraging a culture of lifelong learning to keep pace with AI advancements.
- **Innovation Mindset:** Fostering an environment that embraces experimentation and creativity.
- **Collaboration:** Engaging with partners, stakeholders, and the wider community to drive AI initiatives forward.

12.4 Call to Action for Business Leaders

Business leaders are uniquely positioned to steer their organizations toward successful AI integration:

- **Lead by Example:** Demonstrate commitment to AI adoption and ethical practices.
- **Invest Strategically:** Allocate resources wisely to areas with the highest potential impact.
- **Empower Teams:** Equip employees with the tools and knowledge to leverage AI effectively.

12.5 Final Thoughts

Artificial Intelligence holds immense potential to transform businesses and societies positively. By approaching AI thoughtfully—balancing innovation with responsibility—organizations can unlock new opportunities, drive growth, and contribute to a better future.

Thank you for embarking on this journey through the landscape of AI in business. May the insights and guidance provided in this book empower you to harness the power of AI and lead your organization toward sustained success.

www.ingramcontent.com/pod-product-compliance
Lightning Source LLC
Chambersburg PA
CBHW070115230526
45472CB00004B/1272